ON BIRD HILL

TAY SAFE?

W DO DINOSAURS

Nest Here
th Me

OMPING MONSTERS

MPING MONSTERS

The Girl in the Go

GOO

GOO

ENCE

w fairies

SMOUT & THE LIGHTHOUSE

WAKING DRAGONS

A KITE FOR MOON

HOW DO DINOSAURS SAY GOOD NIGHT?

HOW DO DINOS LEARN TO BE KIND?

THE HORSEBACK Librarians

THE SIMPLE PRINCE

WHAT TO DO WITH A STICK

THE GIANT'S FARM

The Bird of Time

Welcome to the GREEN HOUSE

OFF WE GO!

The Seein

THE BOY W HAD WING

GREYLIN

Love Birds

— animal train —

ONDER UNDERGROUND

Before the

PIGGINS

Mouse's Birthday

Sleeping Beauty

ONCE THERE WAS A STORY

WINGS

TAM LIN

OWL MOON

Eeny Meeny Miney Mole

THE BALLAD OF THE PIRATE QUEENS

HOW DO DINOSAURS CHOOSE THEIR PETS

PICNIC WITH PIGGINS

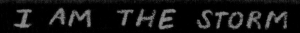

I AM THE STORM

FOR

THE FLYING

ON BALL

SAD, MAD,

SHANKS

HIP HIP

EBIRD

TOO OLD FO

ONE HIPPO H

OPTOAD

PUMPK

BABY BEA BIG DREA

JANIE WRITES
A PLAY

For Janie, who grew up to be my mom.
She continues to inspire me and countless other writers
to tell their great stories. And for Yolanda,
who let me share Janie's story with the world.
—H. E. Y. S.

To my sister, Katie, who has supported and encouraged me
since the day we were born, spending countless hours
reading and creating our own stories that still inspire me.
And to Jane and Heidi, whose books fueled a love for reading
that grew into a lifelong passion for creating picture books.
It is an honor to be a part of this one.
—M. G.

Published by Charlesbridge
9 Galen Street
Watertown, MA 02472
(617) 926-0329
www.charlesbridge.com

Illustrations done in digital media
Display type set in Core Circus 2D In by S-Core Co.
Text type set in Rainier © Kimmy Design
Printed by 1010 Printing International Limited in Huizhou,
    Guangdong, China
Production supervision by Nicole Turner
Designed by Cathleen Schaad

Library of Congress Cataloging-in-Publication Data
Names: Stemple, Heidi E. Y., author. | Goodnight, Madelyn, illustrator.
Title: Janie writes a play / Heidi E. Y. Stemple; illustrated
    by Madelyn Goodnight.
Description: Watertown, MA: Charlesbridge, 2025. | Audience:
    Ages 5–8. | Audience: Grades K–1. | Summary: Dissatisfied with
    the school play, Janie writes a new one—and grows up to be the
    famous author Jane Yolen. Includes biographical note.
Identifiers: LCCN 2023056520 (print) | LCCN 2023056521 (ebook)
    | ISBN 9781623543273 (hardcover) | ISBN 9781632899927
    (ebook)
Subjects: LCSH: Yolen, Jane—Childhood and youth—Juvenile fiction.
    | Authors, American—Childhood and youth—Juvenile fiction.
    | Children's plays—Juvenile fiction. | Creative ability—Juvenile
    fiction. | CYAC: Authors, American—Fiction. | Yolen, Jane—
    Fiction. | Plays—Fiction. | Creative ability—Fiction. | LCGFT:
    Picture books. | Biographical fiction.
Classification: LCC PZ7.1.S7436 Jan 2025 (print) | LCC PZ7.1.S7436
    (ebook) | DDC 813.54 [E]—dc23/eng/20231207
LC record available at https://lccn.loc.gov/2023056520
LC ebook record available at https://lccn.loc.gov/2023056521

Printed in China
(hc) 10 9 8 7 6 5 4 3 2 1

HEIDI E. Y. STEMPLE   ILLUSTRATED BY MADELYN GOODNIGHT

JANIE WRITES A PLAY

JANE YOLEN'S FIRST GREAT STORY

ini Charlesbridge

The night before play rehearsals began, Janie couldn't sleep.

She imagined grand sets and soaring music, exciting dances and catchy songs. And most importantly, a great story.

Janie loved a great story.

Janie grabbed a book from beside her bed.
It was much too old for her, and there were
many words she didn't quite understand.
But she loved the way the words sounded,
even if she didn't know what they meant yet.

She wrote them in her notebook to look
up later.

In the morning, Janie jumped out of bed. She looked out her window, across the street to the park. Anyone else would have seen rocks and trees and people picnicking and taking walks.

But Janie imagined pirates, with cutlasses drawn in fierce battle, on the deck of an ancient galleon. A boy writing a message to the moon on his kite. And a little girl who stomped her huge feet in a dinosaur-sized tantrum.

Before Janie ran out the door, she jotted those story ideas in her notebook.

In the elevator, she told Mr. Schwartz about the play.

Then she handed him the latest copy of the newspaper she and her little brother, Stevie, had written, filled with all the news from their building.

"That'll be five cents," Stevie said
as Mr. Schwartz opened his wallet.

Janie waved hello to the butcher sweeping his front steps as she walked the five blocks to her school, P.S. 93.

"Today's the big day, Janie?" the butcher called out. Janie nodded. She twirled in anticipation of a great story filled with drama and plot twists.

She waited patiently through math and
science and English until finally it was time
to begin the first play rehearsal.

But when she read the script, Janie felt deflated.

"Aren't you excited?" asked Mrs. Jiler.

"You're Girl Number 1! You got the lead role!"

Janie wasn't excited. There was no rising plot or big moment. There was no satisfying ending.

There wasn't any singing or dancing. It wasn't a great story. It wasn't even a good story.

The play was going to be a boring bust.

At the barre in ballet class,
Janie's fondus didn't rise.

Across the floor, her jetés didn't lift.

At the end of class, all the dancers
joined in the center of the room and
danced together.

Everyone.
    Together.
    It made a satisfying ending. A story began
to form in Janie's head. After class, she wrote
it in her notebook.

During dinner, Janie poked at her vegetables. She lined up her carrots and peas in different formations.

When her dad asked what she was doing, she answered distractedly, "Choreography."

Stevie yelled, "Choreogra-peas!"
Everyone laughed.

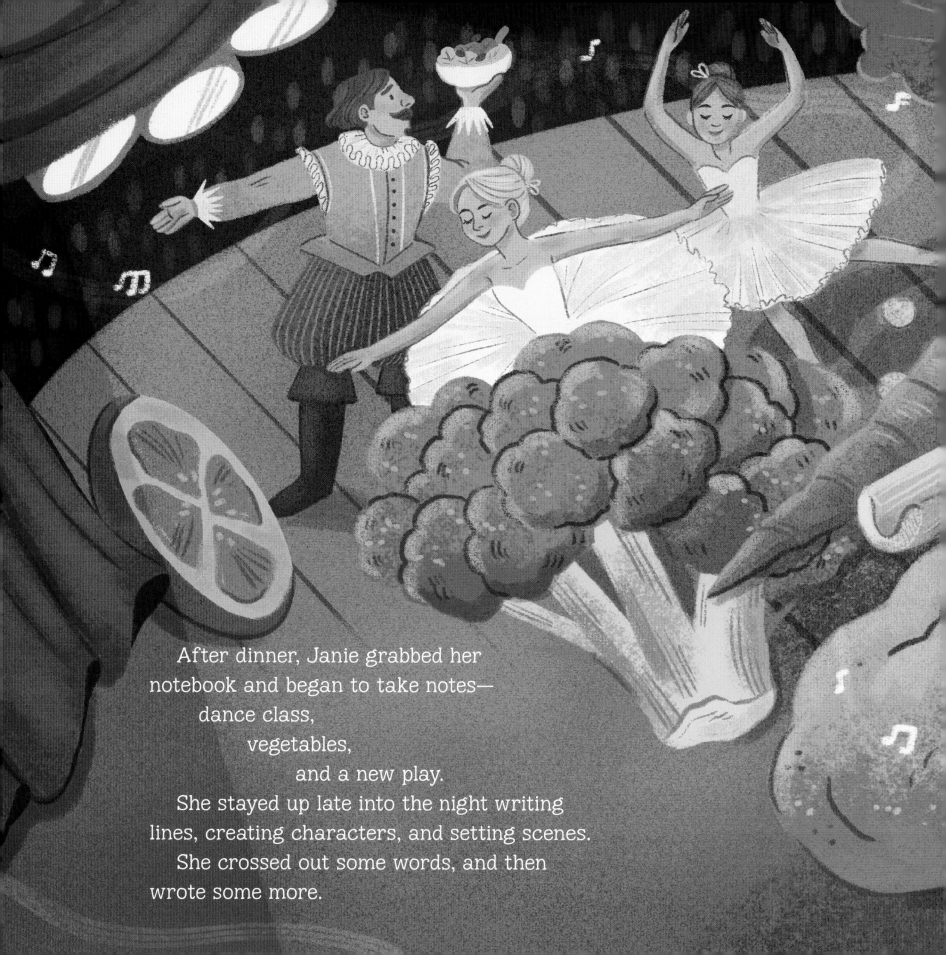

After dinner, Janie grabbed her
notebook and began to take notes—
        dance class,
                vegetables,
                        and a new play.
        She stayed up late into the night writing
lines, creating characters, and setting scenes.
        She crossed out some words, and then
wrote some more.

In the morning, she wasn't tired. She was exhilarated!

In the elevator, Janie was too busy humming a new song from her notebook, so Stevie interviewed Mrs. Schwartz for the newspaper.

Janie danced all the way to P.S. 93.

Mrs. Jiler was confused when Janie handed
her the new script. But she appreciated and
supported her students' work, so she gathered
the class together and handed out new roles.

"Alan and Marcel, you are tomatoes," said Mrs. Jiler.

"Susan H. and Susan L., you are stalks of celery."

"Barbara, Breena, Diane, and Dolores, you are lettuce."

Janie was the chief carrot.

They rehearsed all week.

When the curtains rose on the night of the play,
the audience was respectfully quiet.

They clapped at the beginning of every new scene.

They cheered at the end of every musical number.

When Janie belted out the finale, the audience rose
to their feet in a standing ovation.

It was a great story.

Brava! Bravo! Author, author!

It was Janie's first rave review. It wouldn't be her last.

Janie never stopped loving a great story.
And she never, ever stopped writing.

Now *that's* a satisfying ending.

Author's Note

Little Janie grew up to be Jane Yolen, the famous, award-winning author of more than four hundred books.

As a child, she lived in New York City in an apartment that had fourteen windows overlooking Central Park. Her parents let her read books that she didn't understand yet, some of which are still her favorites today. She and her brother, Steve (who became a journalist), wrote a newspaper, which their mom typed up one copy at a time. Jane and Steve sold copies to their neighbors for five cents.

Jane attended P.S. 93 (Public School 93), and all the students in the story are real. So is Jane's favorite teacher, Mrs. Jiler. Mrs. Jiler always knew that Jane would become a writer. She contacted Jane years later to tell her how proud she was. Jane can't remember the name of the butcher, but she passed his shop each day on her way to school.

The play with the vegetables really did happen. Janie's story and performance as the chief carrot were a smashing success. She still talks about it seventy-five years later.

Did You Notice?

The three books Janie imagined while looking at the people in the park are real books she wrote later. Her first book was called *Pirates in Petticoats*, and she cowrote *A Kite for Moon* with the author of this book. The books in her best-selling How Do Dinosaurs . . . series have become children's classics.

ON BIRD HILL

W DO DINOSAURS TAY SAFE?

Nest Here with Me

OMPING MONSTERS

MPING MONSTERS

The Girl in the Gol...

GOO

...u Fairie's Ball

...JNE

...E HIPPO HOPS

SMOUT & THE LIGHTHOUSE

WAKING DRAGONS

A KITE FOR MOON

HOW DO DINOSAURS SAY GOOD NIGHT?

HOW DO DINOS? LEARN TO BE KIND?

THE HORSEBACK Librarians

THE SIMPLE PRINCE

WHAT TO DO WITH A STICK

THE GIANT'S FARM

The Bird of Time

Welcome to the GREENHOUSE

SEA ...

...FT HOUSE

OFF WE GO!

The Secin...

THE BOY W... HAD WING...

GREYLIA...